Dealing with Loss of a Pet

A Guide to Healing Pet Grief and Losing Your Best Friend

Dealing with the Loss of a Pet

Love Your Life Series

http://loveyourlifeseries.com

ISBN-13:
978-1501054754

ISBN-10:
1501054759

Copyright 2013 by Haven Publishing Group- All rights Reserved

All rights reserved. No part of this book may be reproduced by any mechanical, photographic, or electronic process, or in the form of a phonographic recording; nor may it be stored in a retrieval system, transmitted, or otherwise be copied for public or private use—other than for "fair use" as brief quotations embodied in articles and reviews—without prior written permission of the publisher.

This document is geared towards providing exact and reliable information in regards to the topic and issue covered. The publication is sold with the idea that the publisher is not required to render accounting, officially permitted, or otherwise, qualified services. If advice is necessary, legal or professional, a practiced individual in the profession should be ordered.

The author of this book does not dispense medical advice or prescribe the use of any technique as a form of treatment for physical, emotional, or medical problems without the advice of a physician, either directly or indirectly. The intent of the author is only to offer information of a general nature to help you in your quest for emotional, spiritual and physical well-being. In the event you use any of the information in this book for yourself, which is your constitutional right, the author and the publisher assume no responsibility for your actions. Under no circumstances will any legal responsibility or blame be held against the publisher for any reparation, damages, or monetary loss due to the information herein, either directly or indirectly.

The information herein is offered for informational purposes solely, and is universal as so. The presentation of the information is without contract or any type of guarantee assurance.

The trademarks that are used are without any consent, and the publication of the trademark is without permission or backing by the trademark owner. All trademarks and brands within this book are for clarifying purposes only and are the owned by the owners themselves, not affiliated with this document.

Table Of Contents

Table Of Contents 4

Introduction 5

Keep Up to Date with New Releases 7

Chapter 1 The Stages of Grief 8

Chapter 2 People Who Can Help You Deal with Your Grief 12

Chapter 3 Useful Tips for Overcoming Grief 17

Chapter 4 Moving On with Your Life 22

Steps to Success Action Plan 26

Conclusion 28

Bonus Chapter 29

Other Books you may be interested in 32

Free Gift 33

Introduction

Have you recently lost a loved family member?

Is your pet a part of your family like a child?

Do you struggle daily know that they are gone?

Do you wish you knew how to move through your grief

In this book you will discover the most up-to-date information on dealing with Grief and the Loss of your Beloved Pet.

-What is Grief?

-The Stages of Grief

-Useful tips for overcoming Grief

-Techniques to help you move forward with your life

And much more!

I want to thank you and congratulate you for buying this book, "Dealing with the Loss of a Pet: A Guide to Healing Pet Grief and Losing Your Best Friend!"

I recently lost my beloved Cat, Maggie, she was 16yrs old. I got her in my early teens, and remember having so much fun playing hide and seek with her around the house.... Yes cats do play hide and seek. She was such a big part of my life, and I loved her dearly! I will definitely never forget the little black and white cat the touched my heart.

Grief is hard. Animals are unconditional and always there for you. I hope this book can help to ease your pain, as it has with mine.

Hi There, my name is Simone and I am the creator of the Love you Life Series. Like everyone I have made a few decisions in my life that maybe haven't worked out the way I had planned. But there came a point when I could barely recognize who I was compared with who I wanted to be. Things needed to change!

So I took charge of myself, and made a decision to learn. I pretty much inhaled anything I could that had to do with self –help and I learned the best way for me to let go of the past and move forward with the future was to learn to love myself and my life!

This journey didn't happen overnight, and wasn't done with a one thing fixed all approach, it was like chipping away at a masterpiece a little bit here and a little bit there.

These books have been put together to help you chip away at your masterpiece. It is time to learn to Love Your Life! It is amazing how quickly things will change if we are open to it.

I hope you enjoy this book, and I hope it allows you to start to become the you; you want to be, with the life you want to live.

Keep Up to Date with New Releases

Thank you again for getting yourself a copy of this book Dealing with the Loss of a Pet: A Guide to Healing Pet Grief and Losing Your Best Friend!

I'd like to reward you with this by offering you access to my others books for free by joining my newsletter!

You will be getting up to date information on Personnel Development, Living your happiest life, techniques to become the you, you always wanted to be and you will also get access to other books in the Love your Life Series for free. By joining my newsletter you will be taking a big step forward in being your happiest best Self yet!

Just visit http://loveyourlifeseries.com and get free instant access to the Love Your Life Series newsletter today!

Lastly once you finish reading this book would please review this book on Amazon. With your feedback I continue to make this book better and better.

Thank you!

Chapter 1 The Stages of Grief

Losing your beloved pet is a painful experience. You may be aware that the life span of animals is shorter than that of humans but it still hurts even when you know this fact. It is especially painful if your pet died unexpectedly due to an illness or accident. Mourning is a complex process; it requires time and understanding to help you move on after the painful loss.

This is why you need to learn how to deal with your grief if you want to move on with your life even without your pet by your side. For you to be able to deal with your grief, you need to understand its different stages.

Denial

When you initially heard the bad news that your pet had died, this is the first emotion that you most likely felt. This is the stage wherein you still cannot grasp the idea that your pet is gone forever. You cannot accept the fact that he will not be in your house when you get home from work and you will no longer hear the sound he makes, be it a bark, purr, or tweet. The most important thing about this stage is that it is temporary. You cannot remain in denial for the rest of your life or else you will not be able to move on. Some people stay in denial for a longer period; they only get over it with the help of their loved ones.

This also means feeling numbness and shock because the idea has not yet sunk in. The expected reaction when someone you love dies is sadness and crying over your loss. In most cases, this does not happen until after a few days or weeks because you are still in shock. The denial stage can last for a few days or even weeks after the death.

Anger

Once you finally accept the fact that your pet is gone forever, you will then move on to feeling angry. At this stage, you feel other emotions, too, like sadness, hurt, or panic, but anger is the one that you feel the most. This is one of the few situations wherein getting angry is a good thing. This is when you ask God or someone why they needed to take your pet from you when he was such a sweet little thing who never hurt anyone. You may also feel angry at yourself for not doing enough for your pet, even though you did everything you can.

This emotion may seem irrational to others, especially those who cannot understand what you are going through. They may think that it is a step back from your previous emotions. This is why it is important to understand the stages of grief. At least now, you know that anger is the second stage, and you are in fact progressing rather than falling deeper into despair. Just explain to your loved ones what you are feeling. They will surely understand, especially if they went through the same sad experience sometime in the past.

To manage your anger, you need a kind of outlet wherein you can vent out all your negative feelings. You can call a hotline for people who are dealing with pet grief or speak to a family member or a friend to whom you are really close. You can also punch a pillow or scream into it if it helps relieve the anger. Some people listen to soothing music or take a walk outside to deal with their anger. Do not let the anger get the best of you. Otherwise, it will reach a point wherein it affects your relationships with those who are still living.

Bargaining

This is the stage wherein you bargain for your pet's life. You ask for someone or something that has the power to bring your pet back to life and make everything go back to normal. You pray to God, talk to mediums, and ask your stars or whatever it is that you believe in to bring your pet back. This stage also includes the "what ifs" and "if only" which signify a feeling of guilt. Some owners may feel guilty over the loss of their pets because they think they could have done something about it. Statements like, "What if we didn't leave him alone that day? He might still be alive," and, "If only I had spent more time with him, he could have died happier," suggest that if you could only turn back the hands of time to do things differently for your pet, you would.

Guilt is a natural emotion after losing a pet that you dearly loved. You need to work your way through all these guilt statements before you can finally move on. You need to understand that things happen and there is nothing you can do about it. It is not your fault that your pet died. Besides, you did your best by loving your pet genuinely and wholeheartedly.

Depression

Depression is usually the emotion associated with grief. When you lose a pet, people will think that your first reaction is sadness. Of course you will feel sad upon hearing the news and all throughout the whole experience, but you will only feel real sadness and depression after a few weeks of mourning. This is not the clinical depression that needs professional treatment. Depression in this case only means deep sadness, which is natural considering the fact that you just lost your best friend.

This is the time when you feel hopeless and helpless about the situation. You feel sad whenever you think about your pet. Crying is a good thing for people who are in the process of mourning because it helps them cope with their sadness. When you are feeling a deep sadness, you should not force yourself to go out and meet people. Just give yourself plenty of time to mourn and to cry over your pet. After you have endured several days of depression, you will then feel so much better.

Acceptance

After feeling depressed, you will find yourself snapping out of it and finally learning to accept the fact that your pet is gone and you have no other choice but to move on because you still have a life on which you need to focus. You will know when you are already in the last stage of grief when you are already looking forward instead of backward. Of course you are still remembering special memories with your pet but at the same time, you are looking forward to feeling happy again. When you remember your pet, you do not feel the hurt or sadness but all the happy memories that you have shared together. Once you are in the final stage, you can go back to living your life the way you used to and start your normal routines again.

Note

Understanding the different stages of grief over the loss of a pet will make it easier for you to deal with it. You will know if what you are experiencing is normal or not. If it is normal, you can just continue with the process until you reach the final stage of acceptance. However, if you think your grief is too much and it is affecting your life and your relationship with others negatively, then you might need to seek the help of a counselor.

Chapter 2 People Who Can Help You Deal with Your Grief

When dealing with grief over the loss of your pet, there is a time to be by yourself and there is also a time to be with the people who can help you cope. It is important to seek the help of these people especially if you think your grief is too much for you to bear on your own.

Here is a list of some of the people in your life and some professionals who can help you deal with grief after your pet had died.

Family members

If you are still living with your family, they will also be affected by the death of your pet, especially if he was a family pet. Even if you considered yourself as the pet owner, the other members of the household surely feel the same pain and sadness. You can talk to your family members about what you are feeling. They are the ones who will understand you and what you are going through better than anyone because they are experiencing the same thing. If you are the head of the family, it is best to gather all the family members and have a talk where you can share your feelings and emotions about what happened. It is important to stick together in times like this. It would feel as if you have lost a child or a sibling because your pet has become a part of your family.

Even if you do not live with your family and you are the sole pet owner, you can still go to your family for comfort. You can go to your parents' house and stay in your old room just to feel safe and secure. Your parents will surely understand what you are going through and they will be happy to help any way they can. If you have a sibling with whom you have a close relationship, you can also ask him or her to visit or you can visit him or her yourself just to have a family member with you in your time of grieving.

Close friends

Your close friends should also be at the top of your list of people whom you can talk to when dealing with grief over the loss of your pet. Your close friends are also like family, especially if you live alone and your family is miles away. You can turn to your close friends for comfort.

It is best to talk to someone who has experienced losing a pet. If you have close friends who have been in the kind of situation that you are experiencing now, you can express your feelings with them and they will know what to do because they have experienced the same thing. If you do not have a close friend who experienced losing a pet, you can contact someone who owns a pet. Pet owners can easily sympathize and empathize with their fellow pet owners because they understand the deep love and friendship that bonds pets and owners together. They may not have any experience dealing with the loss of a pet but it is not that difficult for them to imagine the pain and sadness that you are going through.

Even if your close friends do not have pets, you can always turn to them for comfort. After all, what are friends for than being people you can turn to in times of need? Your friends can surely be trusted to provide you with comfort whether they are pet owners or not.

Your pet's vet

If you have befriended your pet's veterinarian in the years that you and your pet visited him for vaccinations, checkups, and treatments, you can also talk to him to help you deal with your grief. The vet will know your pet's behavior and quirks, which will make it easier for you to remember without feeling sad. Some considerate vets even give souvenirs to pet owners like a framed paw print or a certificate for animals.

If for no other reason than simply wanting to get answers to all the questions in your mind, you can go to your pet's vet and ask for an explanation. The vet can assure you that your pet did not have to undergo too much pain before he died or that the death is something that cannot be avoided and no one is to blame for it. The vet can also tell you small but meaningful details that can affect how you will move on later like the way your pet smiled sweetly before passing away. Knowing these things will give you the peace of mind you need to help you move on with your life more easily.

Pet loss hotline

There are also hotlines available to people who are dealing with the loss of a pet. This is ideal for owners who recently lost pets and need to talk to someone as soon as possible. Some people find it more comfortable to talk to a stranger than to someone who knows them about their feelings over the death of their beloved pet.

To find a pet loss support hotline, you can check your telephone directory and look under the "pets" or "support hotlines" listings. You can also check online for different pet loss support hotlines that serve your area. People who answer calls from pet owners know what they need to do. They know how to handle the different emotions that the pet owner is feeling like denial, anger, guilt, and sadness over the loss of a pet because they have been trained for dealing with these kinds of calls.

They know what to say and when to say it, which will make you feel much better, even for just a short time.

Pet loss support group

If you need to be with people who share the same pain and sadness over the loss of a pet, you can join a pet loss support group. The members of this group are pet owners who have experienced losing a pet. Some of them may be like you who are still in the process of healing while others have already healed and just want to be an inspiration to their fellow pet owners by sharing their own experiences. You can talk to the other members and share what you are feeling without being embarrassed about it because you know that they have felt or are feeling the same way.

If you are a member of an organization of animal lovers, your friends can give you some recommendations on where you can find a pet loss support group. Or maybe your group organizes these kinds of meetings for their members who lost their own pets. You should join these meetings where you can vent out and express your feelings without worrying about being judged and ridiculed.

Counselor

If you think your depression is getting worse and it is affecting your relationship with your loved ones and other aspects of your life, you should consider going to a counselor for help. There are grief counseling sessions available to people who recently lost loved ones or even pets. These counselors can give you professional help and advice on how to overcome your grief as well as some much-needed comfort. Grief counseling is offered by psychiatrists who specialize in dealing with grief after the loss of a loved one or any other traumatic event that caused grief. Counseling is not free of charge; you have to pay the psychiatrist's fee for the services. Make sure that you choose someone who has a good reputation in your area. You do not want to waste your hard-earned money on a bogus counselor especially in your time of mourning.

Chapter 3 Useful Tips for Overcoming Grief

People deal with grief in different ways with only one thing in mind—to let go of their pain and sadness and to remember only the good memories that they shared with their pets so that they can move on with their lives. It is important to know how to deal with grief the right way to make it easier for you to live your life the way you used to before losing your pet.

Here are some useful tips that you can try to help you overcome your grief over a pet that you recently lost.

Embrace the emotions

As what was discussed in the previous chapters, you will feel different emotions after losing your beloved companion. These emotions are all part of coping with grief and it is normal to feel all these emotions. The only time you have to worry is when you are wallowing too much in one particular feeling, like being in denial or depression for more than a year. Once you feel these emotions, you need to let go of yourself and just embrace the feeling. It is best to just allow yourself to grieve rather than keep pretending that you are not affected because you are only prolonging your grief. It may sound contradictory, but it is important to give yourself enough time to grieve if you want to get over your grief as soon as possible.

Spend time alone

Your loved ones may think that you need constant companionship after losing a pet. This is not exactly true especially in the first few weeks after your pet's death. In the first few weeks, it is best to just stay at home by yourself where you can reminisce all the good times that you shared with your pet. You can look at his pictures, browse through his toys, and just cry whenever you feel like it. When you are constantly with friend's right after you lost your pet, you will be forced to be happy even when you just want to cry deep down because you do not want them to worry about you. It is also better if you just stay at home because you will be no fun at parties, though it is totally understandable since you just lost a pet. When your friends ask you to go out with them, just politely say "no" and tell them that you would rather be alone. Your friends mean well so do not take it against them if they seem a bit "pushy" in trying to cheer you up.

Be busy

You should also keep yourself busy by doing your favorite pastime or starting a new hobby. This is after the first few days of crying and reminiscing and you still do not feel like going out and mingling with friends. You can finish the sewing project that you have been putting off for the longest time now or you can start learning something that you have not tried before like crocheting. Choose hobbies that are simple and do not require too much physical exertion. This is because you still feel drained from all the emotions that you felt in the past few days or weeks. Quiet hobbies like cross stitching or crocheting will put your mind at ease even for just a few minutes each day.

Explain your situation to your boss

If you are having a hard time coping with grief and it is affecting your job, you should explain your situation to your boss. This does not mean that you are using the death of your pet as an excuse for your failure to do your job properly. You are doing this because it is only fair for your boss and coworkers to know what is going on so that they can make the necessary adjustments. If you think you need a break from work, you should go ahead and ask your boss to give you some vacation time. He or she may even suggest that you take a vacation if he or she knows your situation, which is why it is best to be honest with him or her about what you are going through.

Talk to your loved ones

The previous chapter gives you a list of people whom you can talk to while you are mourning for your pet. Once you start to come to terms with your loss, you can now start talking about it to your loved ones. You can tell them about your feelings or you can share funny stories about your pet. These people love you and they know how you must be feeling. They will do everything they can to listen and empathize with what you are experiencing right now.

Do physical activities

When you no longer feel too drained because of all the emotions, you can now start doing physical activities like jogging, working out at the gym, yoga, and exercise to name a few. For some people, doing strenuous activities that require a lot of energy helps them cope with grief. This is because they are putting all their energy into the activity, which gives them very little time to cry or feel sad. After doing a particularly strenuous exercise and you suddenly remember your pet, you will only say that you are too tired to cry or you no longer have the energy to feel sad and hurt.

Do something in memory of your pet

You can have a memorial service as a way to remember your pet before putting him in his final resting place.

This also allows your family members who also loved your pet dearly to share their feelings. Having a memorial service is a way for those who are left behind to celebrate the life that the animal shared with them.

Aside from having a memorial, you can do something else in memory of your pet like planting a tree and naming it after him or building a small statue in your garden where he loved to play. Some pet owners even go as far as having the bodies of their pets preserved via taxidermy, although a lot of people find this a little extreme and morbid for their taste. It is up to you how you want to remember your pet once he is gone. After all, you are the pet owner and the one who feels pain and sadness more than anyone.

Helping a child deal with losing a pet

If your child is the main owner of your family pet, you do not just think about dealing with your own grief but also your child's grief. Children may have a hard time coping with the loss of their pet because they are still too young to understand what really happened. It is your responsibility as a parent or as an adult to explain to your child what happened.

If your pet had to undergo euthanasia, you should explain to your child what euthanasia is and why it is necessary. Give your child a chance to say goodbye to your pet before the euthanasia is administered.

You do not have to pretend that you are not affected by the loss of your family pet in front of your child. In fact, it is better if you let your child see that you are also grieving. This will make your child feel that it is okay to cry and feel sad. You should also explain to your child that grieving is only a sign that he or she cares deeply and has compassion for animals.

Reassure your child that it is nobody's fault and that your pet is in a better place now. This will make the child feel at ease because he or she knows that your pet is doing well wherever he is.

Chapter 4 Moving On with Your Life

After the whole process of grieving, you are now ready to move on with your life. Moving on is important because it allows you to go back to living your life the way you used to. Some people can easily move on after just a few weeks while others take several months before they can finally move on. Whether it took you a long or a short time before you finally moved on from mourning the death of your pet, the most important thing is that you are finally ready to let go of the past and start a new life. Here the signs that will tell you and other people that you have moved on.

You can talk about your pet without breaking down

During the first few months, it will be difficult for you to talk about your pet without bursting into tears. However, as time goes by, you will realize that you can now talk about your beloved animal companion without feeling any pain or sadness. In fact, when you talk about your pet, the first things that come to mind are your happy memories, like the way he used to lick your face to wake you up in the morning or how he used to love eating fruits and vegetables rather than dog food. This makes it easier for your friends to talk to you about your pet because they now know that you are okay with it.

Years have passed

Although there is no real time frame for grieving or moving on, it is most likely that you have already moved on after, say, five years. When it comes to grieving, the proverb "Time heals all wounds" rings true. This varies from person to person because some may take a long time to grieve while others only need a few days. However, it is safe to say that after several years, you will have finally moved on with your life.

You do not constantly think about your pet

In the first few weeks after losing your pet, you will find yourself thinking about him all the time—when you wake up in the morning, while doing your daily habits and routine, and before going to sleep. However, as the days pass, you will find yourself not thinking about your pet as often as you used to. This does not mean that you have forgotten about him, though; it only means that you have finally moved on with your life.

You remember good memories

Another sign that you have finally moved on is when your pet's death is just a blurred event in the past and what you can remember vividly are your fun moments together. In the first few days or weeks after your pet's death, you cannot think about even the happy times without crying. This will change as you move farther away from the time of your pet's death.

Tips for moving on

There are some things that you will be ready to do once you have finally moved on. The list below will give you some ideas on what you can do once you have finally gone past your grief.

Sort through your pet's belongings

It is easy to sort through your pet's belongings because he only had a few. You can now ask yourself what you are going to do with his house, bed, collars, and clothes (if he had any). You can always keep these things in the attic or garage as souvenirs but for some pet owners, they prefer to get rid of their pets' things in so that it will be easier for them to move on. You can donate your pet's belongings to an animal shelter or just simply throw them away when the garbage collector arrives. You can also sell them along with your other old stuff when you organize a yard sale. However, if your pet had a disease, which was the main cause of his death, you need to properly dispose of his belongings as soon as possible.

Volunteer

Another great idea is to volunteer in different animal organizations. There are so many organizations out there that are dedicated to the welfare of animals. Choose a group in your area to make it easier for you to volunteer. You can volunteer in an animal shelter where there are stray dogs that are up for adoption. There are also non-profit organizations that fight against cruelty to animals in any way, shape, or form. In any case, joining a charity group or an animal rights organization is a sign that you have finally moved on with your life. This shows that you are finally past your grief and are now ready to take action to start a new life and do something in memory of your pet.

To choose the right non-profit organization, you should consider the advocacy that is closest to your heart. If your pet died from an illness, you can volunteer for a group that helps pets who have this illness and are in need of medical attention. If your pet was a beagle, you can volunteer in an organization that promotes the welfare of beagles.

Get back in circulation

Once you have finally moved on, you are now ready to get back in circulation and simply have fun without feeling guilty. You can go out with friends and go to parties. This is the perfect time to reconnect with friends and rebuild your social life. By this time, your pet's death is an event of the past and all you have now are happy memories that you will always carry with you in your heart. You can even organize a party at home as a way to thank your friends and loved ones who helped you deal with one of the saddest events in your life.

Go back to work

If you took a break from work because of your loss, you can now go back to work because you are mentally and emotionally ready. Once you have moved on, you can start doing your tasks more efficiently. You will be more productive because you no longer feel the hurt and sadness that you felt in the first few weeks of grieving. Your boss and colleagues will be glad that you are back on the job and in your normal self again.

Consider getting a new pet

You can now think about getting a new pet without feeling guilty about it or as if you are being disloyal to your pet. It is important to do this once you are sure that you are ready. You should not get another pet as an instant replacement or as a way for you to ease the pain. Otherwise, you are only making it worse for yourself because you will not be able to completely move on. It is also unfair to the new pet because you will not be giving him your full love and attention. It may take several months or even years before you consider getting another pet again. Even if it takes you a long time to move on, you should still be open to the idea of getting a new pet because you have a big heart that loves and cares deeply for animals.

Steps to Success Action Plan

Steps to Success has been put together to give you somewhere to start with your grief at such a hard time.

To really have success you may need to use this action plan a few times and trial a few different things to get the result you're after. Test, Measure and Monitor needs to become your motto until you are having happier days again. Grief is hard, and the pain will start to lessen, although it may never entirely go away.

Step 1- Read this book from the beginning and take notes or highlight the things that stand out.

Step 2- Take a good look at yourself and realize which stage of grief you are at right now. By doing this stage you can be better mentally prepared for the next stages.

Step 3 –Be vocal about what you are going through. Minimizing your loss and treating it like just another thing that happened won't help you. You need to talk and share with people you trust. Let it all out! It is also ok to physically let it out. If you need to cry, cry, if you need to punch something, find a punching bag. Be gentle on yourself and allow yourself some time to heal.

Step 4 –Create a plan for remembering your pet… would you like to create a memorial site for your pet, or dedicate a photo album to your pet. Spending some time thinking about how you would like to remember your pet is important as is will help you to start moving forward.

Step 5 –Remember that grieving takes time! Do not rush yourself, or tell yourself you should be over it. Be easy on yourself!

Conclusion

Thank you for buying this book!

I hope this book was able to help you in this sad time.

The next step is to use the Steps to Success, and start trying to move forward, taking each day one day at a time.

Finally, if you enjoyed this book, please take the time to share your thoughts and post a review on Amazon. It'd be greatly appreciated!

Thank you and good luck!

http://loveyourlifeseries.com

Bonus Chapter

This Bonus Chapter is from the book The Secret to Being Happy Now: 12 Simple Steps to a Happy New You Today! Enjoy!

Choosing Happiness

When someone asks you what you want to achieve, you will probably have a lot of things to say. Still it all boils down to one thing – you want to be happy. If there is one thing that every person here on Earth has in common, it is the desire to live a happy life.

It is a human need to hold happiness in our hands. You spend every moment of every day of your whole life for it. It makes the world go round. It is important as the air that keeps us alive. Nobody wants to get to old age with regrets, learning to live a Happy life in the here and now is arguably the biggest goal you can set for yourself!

However there can be certain times in your life when Happiness is a little bit harder to find. You may be having trouble at work, or in your relationships. You may be struggling financially, or you just might be sad. Happiness is not something that can be brought and used, you will go through ups and downs in your life and you need to accept where you are at, at any given time. But that doesn't mean you can't work towards being happier.

Happiness is a choice, and you can make the choice to stay were you are, or you make the choice to be responsible for your own Happiness and start working towards being Happier. Happiness is like a muscle, it will get stronger the more you work the muscle, or the more you focus on trying to be happy. Decide not to settle for anything less than a Happy life and you will find if you focus on your happiness you will start to turn things around!

The Big Things

You could say you want to be rich and get onto the Forbes' Wealthiest. You could say you want to be famous and have a smash hit world tour. You could also say you want to own a posh house and live a luxurious life in Beverly Hills.

There are things that you are willing to work hard for in order to get it, the things that you know will make you happy. These are things you live for, the reason why you wake up and work hard everyday. These are the things that keep you going.

The big things will always be the light at the end of the tunnel. It will push you to go on no matter how dark the tunnel seems to be. It is called goals, often, dreams. This is the kind of happiness that generates hope and faith that something good will come your way.

With this kind of Happiness you can feel a sense of pride that you are doing something pro-active and a sense of achievement when you get what you want. Having Goals can be a really easy way to improve your happiness, because the more you chip away at them, the more self confidence you will have, and the happier you will be in yourself!

The Little Things

They say the best things in life are the little things because they actually make up the big things. It may not be true all the time, but it often is. When you look around you, it may take some time, but you will see that happiness can be made by the little things.

An 8-hour sleep, a bus that arrived on time, the pair of shoes you want on sale, not getting into traffic, the beauty of the street after the rain, an all-day road trip, a good book – these are the little things that light up your day.

Unlike the big things, these little things are the spice of your everyday life. These are the things that make you feel alive on a day to day basis. It is the candle that you hold on to as you walk through the dark tunnel.

It doesn't matter that if you haven't achieved what you wanted to for the day or for the week for that matter. Happiness is everywhere. We live on a beautiful planet with so many beautiful things, and you can change your mood to happy just by being a little bit grateful for some of those smaller things.

Whether it is a small thing or a big thing, the secret of life is to appreciate it before it is gone. Nothing in life will stay forever so enjoy each and every thing that you have before it's too late.

To check out the rest of this book The Secret to Being Happy Now: 12 Simple Steps to a Happy New You Today! Just go to Amazon.com

Other Books you may be interested in...

Below you'll find some of my other books currently available through Amazon. There are currently over 20 Love Your Life Series Books available so stay tuned to the website, social media and Amazon for more brilliant titles from the Love Your Life Series.

The Secret to Being Happy Now: 12 Simple Steps to a Happy New You Today!

Mindset Solutions: Create Your Ultimate Life by Changing Your Mind!

Ultimate EFT: Emotional Freedom Technique made Easy to clear your Beliefs and Change your Life

You can simply search for these amazing titles on the Amazon website.

Free Gift

Thank you for reading this Book Dealing with the Loss of a Pet: A Guide to Healing Pet Grief and Losing Your Best Friend!

I'd like to reward you with this by offering you access to my others books for free by joining my newsletter!

You will be getting up to date information on Personnel Development, Living your happiest life, techniques to become the you, you always wanted to be and you will also get access to other books in the Love your Life Series for free. By joining my newsletter you will be taking a big step forward in being your happiest best Self yet!

Just visit http://loveyourlifeseries.com and get free instant access to the Love your Life Series newsletter today!

Lastly once you finish reading this book would please review this book on Amazon. With your feedback I continue to make this book better and better.

Thank you

Printed in Great Britain
by Amazon